Contents

KB095661

 **1. Family**

 A **Words to Know**

Highlight the words you know.

Target Words			
family	grandfather	grandmother	parent
father	mother	brother	sister
son	daughter	uncle	aunt
cousin	husband	wife	baby

 B **Family Tree**

Meet a family. Look and write.

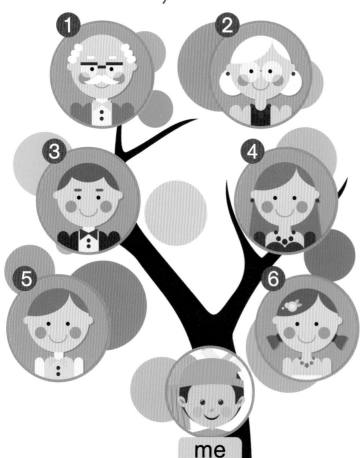

1. grand _ _ _ _ _ _

2. gr _ _ _ mother

3. f _ th _ _

4. mo _ _ er

5. br _ _ _ _ _

6. si _ _ er

me

2 Word POP

C Family Album

Look through the photos. Find and write.

family

parent

son

husband

wife

baby

1.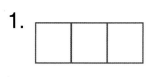

2.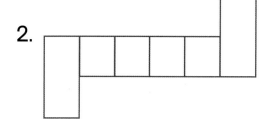

3.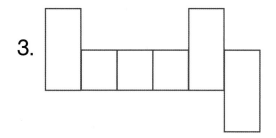

4.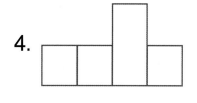

5.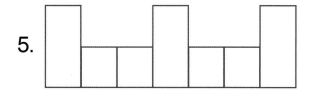

6.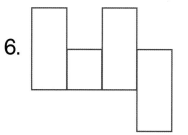

D Word Maze

Begin at the red flag and find the family words. Circle and write.

1.

_____

2.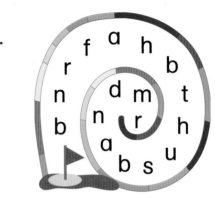

_____

3.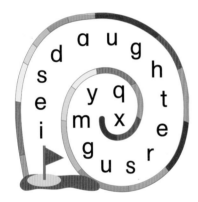

_____

4.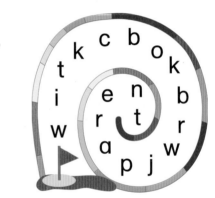

_____

5.

_____

6.

_____

We are going to see our grandmother and grandfather.

 A Family Trip

Marci's family is going to see their grandparents.
Read and circle the family words.

My father is driving. My mother is singing to my younger sister, Darcie. We are all happy. We are on our way to Florida. We are going to see our grandmother and grandfather.

 B Write Right!

Unscramble and write.

| are going to | our grandmother |
| We | and grandfather. | see |

2. Weather & Seasons T2

A Words to Know

Highlight the words you know.

Target Words			
seasons	spring	summer	fall
winter	weather	warm	cool
hot	cold	sunny	windy
rainy	cloudy	stormy	snowy

Day 3

B Seasons Change

Follow the weather and seasons. Look and write.

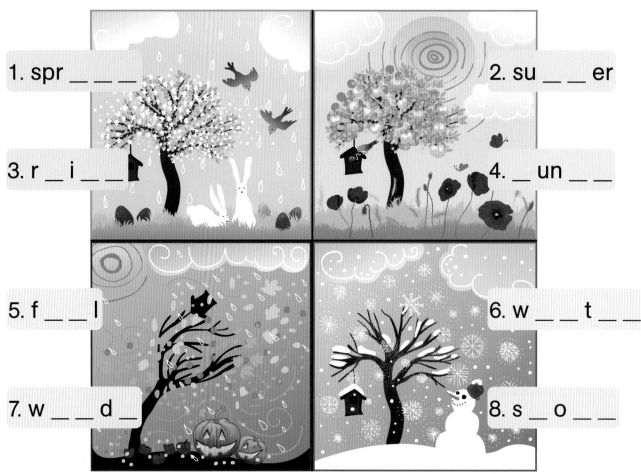

1. spr _ _ _

2. su _ _ er

3. r _ i _ _ _

4. _ un _ _

5. f _ _ l

6. w _ _ t _ _

7. w _ _ d _

8. s _ o _ _

C Word Hunt

Look at the pictures through a magnifying glass.
Look and choose.

1.

| hot |
| warm |
| cold |

2.

| winter |
| fall |
| spring |

3.

| windy |
| sunny |
| cloudy |

4.

| stormy |
| snowy |
| sunny |

D Weather Forecaster

Complete the chart as a weather forecaster.

Mon.	Tues.	Wed.	Thurs.	Fri.

Word Bank

cloudy   stormy   rainy   sunny   windy

E Picture Code

Break the code to find the weather and seasons. Find and write.

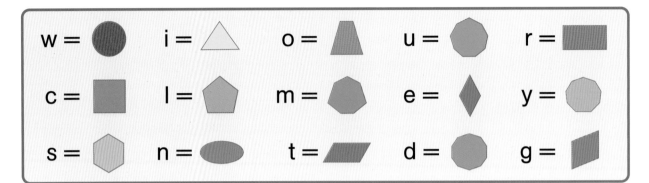

w = ●	i = △	o = ▲	u = ⬡	r = ▬
c = ■	l = ⬠	m = ⬡	e = ◆	y = ⬢
s = ⬡	n = ⬭	t = ▱	d = ⬢	g = ▰

Day 4

1.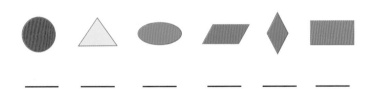

    ___ ___ ___ ___ ___ ___

2.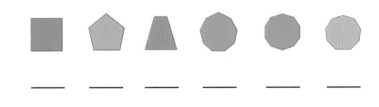

    ___ ___ ___ ___ ___ ___

3.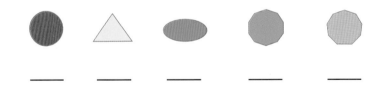

    ___ ___ ___ ___ ___

4.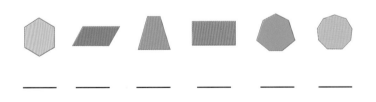

    ___ ___ ___ ___ ___ ___

5.

    ___ ___ ___ ___ ___

What is your favorite season?
Spring is my favorite season.

A Four Seasons

Talk about seasons with friends. Look and write.

1.

_____ is
my favorite season.

2.

_____ is
my favorite season.

3.

_____ is
my favorite season.

4.

_____ is
my favorite season.

B How About You?

What is your favorite season?

_____ is my _____ _____.

A Angry Letters

Calm down the letters. Unscramble and write.

1.  h w e t a e r

_____

2.  h r a e g d u t

_____

3.  o y s m t r

_____

4.  a s n s e o s

_____

5.  grafnadthre

_____

6.  n i c s u o

_____

B Odd One Out

Find the different word. Read and circle.

1. summer   son   hot   cold

2. spring   summer   snowy   fall

3. baby   mother   father   cloudy

4. husband   cool   cold   hot

Day 5

C A Slip of the Tongue

Find the words that are not right! Look and correct.

1.

My favorite season is ~~fall~~. The sun is hot. The trees are green.

| fall | → | summer |

2.

Bobby is very happy because of the surprise from his grandmother.

| | → | |

3.

Once upon a time, there was a woman with seven uncles and one daughter.

| | → | |

4.

It is stormy again! Hurray! I can ride my new bike now.

| | → | |

Word Bank

grandfather   sunny   sons   summer

3. Food

A Words to Know

Highlight the words you know.

Day 1

Target Words

food	beef	bread	cake
chicken	cookie	egg	hot dog
milk	pizza	rice	sandwich
soup	spaghetti	yogurt	

B Delicious Food

Throw a party! Look and write.

1. s _ _ d _ _ _ h

2. y _ _ _ _ t

3. c _ _ _

4. m _ l _

5. s _ _ _ _ _ _ _ _ _

6. c _ o _ _ e

7. _ i _ e

8. _ ee _

C Messy Menu

Unscramble the mixed up menu. Look and write.

MENU

1. aipzz

2. osup

3. hpgseatti

4. bdera

5. cier

6. efbe

7. kechnic

8. eoiock

9. uygrot

D Cookie Crumbs

Clean up your textbook. Find and write.

1. ri  e
     ookie
    sandwi  h

     is letter ☐ .
    ♡

2. pizz
    bre  d
    sp  ghetti

     is letter ☐ .
    🐚

3. mil
    chic  en
    coo  ie

     is letter ☐ .
    🐚

4.  gg
    be  f
    chick  n

     is letter ☐ .
    ☆

I want ___ ___ ___ ___ !
♡   🐚   🐚   ☆

We need some milk and eggs.

A At the Supermarket

Sam and his mother are shopping at the supermarket.
Look and choose.

1.

   a. We need some fruits and vegetables.

   b. We need some milk and eggs.

2.

   a. We need some pizza and soup.

   b. We need some beef and chicken.

B Write Right!

Look and write.

"We need some _____."

4. Fruits & Vegetables

A Words to Know

Highlight the words you know.

Target Words

fruits	apple	banana	grapes	melon
orange	peach	pear	strawberry	
watermelon	vegetables	bean	cabbage	
carrot	cucumber	onion	potato	pumpkin

B In the Refrigerator

Look at the fruits and vegetables. Look and write.

1. o _ _ on

2. _ a _ _ a _ _

3. p _ _ r

4. m _ _ _ n

5. g _ _ _ _ s

C Shopping Trip

Check the shopping list. Write only the words on the list.

Shopping List

carrot   potato
grapes   watermelon
cucumber   strawberry

1.  _____

2.  _____

3.  _____

4.  _____

5.  _____

6.  _____

7.  _____

8.  _____

■ Write two more fruits that you like!

_____   _____

D Word Search

Read across and down. Find and circle.

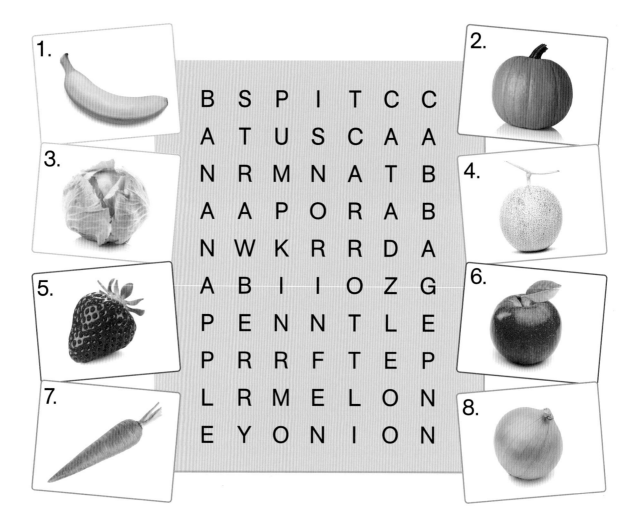

Write the words in lowercase.

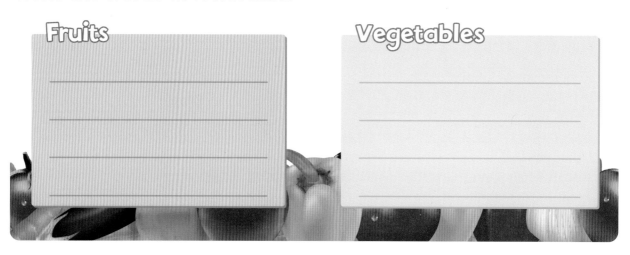

I don't like cucumbers.

A Whose Line Is It?

May and her mother are talking over breakfast. Find and write.

1. _____

2. _____

Sentence Bank

I don't like cucumbers.   Eat your vegetables.

B Write Right!

Unscramble and write.

| like | I | cucumbers. | don't |

A Something Smells Good!

Look at what they are cooking. Check and trace.

Day 5

1.

☐ cookies
☐ yogurt

2.

☐ bread
☐ spaghetti

3.

☐ hot dog
☐ sandwich

4.

☐ pizza
☐ rice

B Angry Letters

Calm down the letters. Unscramble and write.

1. c t r o a r

_____

2. c a b g b e a

_____

3. h p c e a

_____

4. p r e a

_____

C Helping Out

Sam is helping his mother at the supermarket. Find and write.

1. "First, let's get some _____ cakes," Mom says.

2. "Now we need some _____ and _____s," Mom says.

3. "Mom, do we need some _____ and chicken?" Sam asks.

    "Yes, Sam. We do need some meat," Mom says.

4. "Do we need some _____s?" Sam asks.

    "Yes, we do need some fruits and vegetables," Mom says.

Word Bank

apple   milk   beef   rice   egg

5. Action Verbs

A Words to Know

Highlight the words you know.

Target Words

chase	come	crawl	dance	drink
eat	fly	go	hop	jump
kick	point	pull	push	run
sing	sit down	stand up	walk	

Day 1

B Play Time

Look at the pictures. Look and write.

1. __ l __

2. j __ m __

3. c __ __ wl

4. st __ __ __ up

5. s __ __ d __ w __

6. p __ __ l

7. s __ n __

C Picture Pieces

Look at the puzzle pieces. Trace, find, and write.

1. crawl ☐

2. jump ☐

3. dance ☐

4. drink ☐

5. run ☐

6. sit down ☐

7. push ☐

8. chase ☐

a

b

c

d

e

f

g

h

D Fruit Hunt

Circle the fruits only. Write the words.

I can fly with the bees.

A Happy Bird

Duck and Peacock are saying hello to each other.
Read and choose.

"Hello, Peacock," shouts Duck.

"Hello, Duck. How are you today?" asks Peacock.

"I am a happy bird! I ⎹ can ⎹ cannot ⎹ fly with the bees,"
says Duck happily.

"I am not a happy bird. I ⎹ can ⎹ cannot ⎹ fly with the bees.
My, oh my! I want to fly with the bees," says Peacock sadly.

B Read Again!

What does Duck say? Find and write.

" I am a happy bird! I can _____ "

6. Appearance & People

T8

A Words to Know

Highlight the words you know.

Target Words

bald	beautiful	handsome	fat	thin
pretty	noisy	quiet	old	young
tall	short	strong	weak	children
boy	girl	man	woman	

B Meet People

Look at the people. Look and write.

1. ch _ _ d _ _ _

2. _ h _ _ t

3. t _ _ _

4. _ l _

5. y _ _ n _

6. g _ _ _

7. _ _ y

C Word Split

Connect each picture to the right word. Match and trace.

1.  2.  3.  4.

nois wo chil qui

dren et y man

D Word Pattern

Find the pattern. Read and write.

1. fat - fat - thin - fat - fat - thin - fat - _____ - _____

2. old - young - old - young - old - _____

3. tall - tall - short - short - tall - tall - _____ - _____

Find the words that match the pictures.
Do the math and write them.

1.  — wo =

2. fl + — bo =

3.  — irl + o =

4.  — k + ther =

5. l +  — str =

Word Bank

woman   boy   weak   girl   strong

The turnip falls on the old man.

A Pull Together

They are pulling out the big, giant turnip. Read and circle the people words.

The turnip falls on the old man. The old man falls on the old woman. The old woman falls on the girl. The girl falls on the dog. The dog falls on the cat.

B Write Right!

Unscramble and write.

man.	on	The turnip	the	falls	old

A Angry Letters

Calm down the Letters. Unscramble and write.

1. c e a n d _____

2. t p n i o _____

3. w c a r l _____

4. c e m o _____

5. i s n o y _____

6. c s a h e _____

Day 5

B About My Friends

Describe Jenny and Nate.

1. Nate is a h_____ boy.

2. He is _____ and _____.

3. Jenny is a p_____ girl.

4. She is _____ and _____.

Word Bank

pretty   handsome   tall   short   strong   thin

C Word Hunt

Look at the picture frame. Read and choose.

1.

fly	walk	crawl
	come	

2.

come	drink	hop
	go	

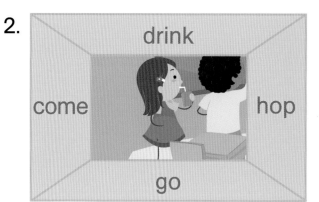

3.

weak	noisy	quiet
	pretty	

4.

point	push	kick
	pull	

5.

kick	point	push
	pull	

6.

short	tall	weak
	strong	

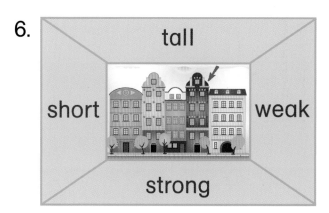

7. Opposites

A Words to Know

Highlight the words you know.

<table>
<tr><th colspan="7">Target Words</th></tr>
<tr><td>good</td><td>bad</td><td>big</td><td>little</td><td></td><td>clean</td><td>dirty</td></tr>
<tr><td>fast</td><td>slow</td><td>hard</td><td>soft</td><td></td><td>heavy</td><td>light</td></tr>
<tr><td>high</td><td>low</td><td>huge</td><td>tiny</td><td></td><td>long</td><td>short</td></tr>
<tr><td>rich</td><td>poor</td><td>same</td><td>different</td><td></td><td></td><td></td></tr>
</table>

B Opposite Cards

Think of the opposite words. Look and write.

1.

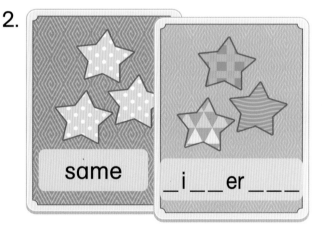

f _ s _ | slow

2.

same | _ i _ _ er _ _ _ _

3.

dirty | c _ _ _ _ n

4.

l _ t _ l _ | big

Day 1

C Opposite Match

Read the 8 sets of opposite words. Look and write.

1.
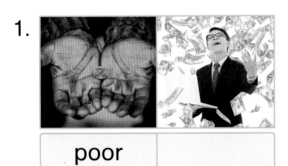

poor	

2.

	clean

3.

	low

4.
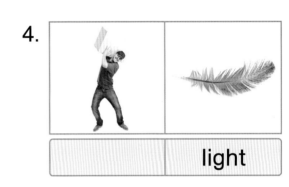

	light

5.
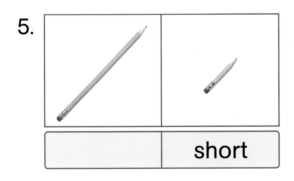

	short

6.

hard	

7.
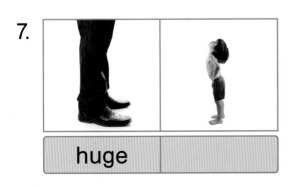

huge	

8.

good	

Common Letters

Search for the shared letter. Find and write.

1.

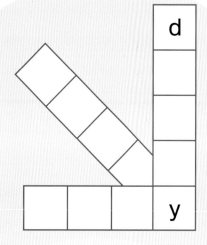

2.

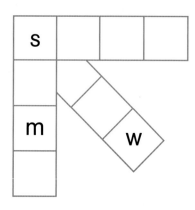

3.

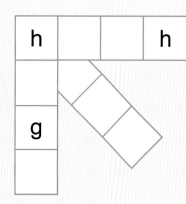

4.

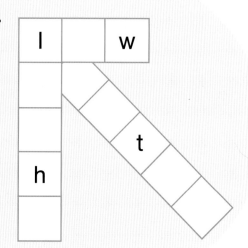

Day 2

Word Bank

huge	heavy	same	dirty	tiny	high
slow	hard	soft	light	little	low

I have short arms. I have little hands.

A They Are Different!

Vinnie is different from his grandparents. Look and write.

1. Grandfather has long arms. His arms reach the top of the bookshelf. I have _____ arms. My arms reach only the bottom of the bookshelf.

2. Grandmother has big hands. Her hands hold three oranges. I have _____ hands. My hands hold only one orange.

B Opposite Pairs

Complete the chart.

	My Grandparents	Me
1.	Grandfather has long arms.	
2.	Grandmother has big hands.	

8. Colors

A Words to Know

Highlight the words you know.

Target Words

colors	black	blue	brown
gray	green	orange	pink
purple	red	white	yellow
colorful			

B Colorful Fish

Visit the colorful underwater world. Look and write.

1. b _ a _ _

2. _ e _ _ o _

3. or _ _ _ e

4. _ l _ e

5. w _ _ te

6. br _ _ _

Day 3

C Fruit Stand Picture

Look at all the colors. Choose and write.

yellow   purple   pink

red   green   blue

orange   white

_____   _____

_____   _____

_____   _____

D Color Word Search

Find the words and check.

b	l	a	c	k	m
l	r	x	v	a	g
u	n	o	n	p	r
e	s	q	w	i	a
g	r	e	e	n	y
b	x	t	o	k	g

☐ gray   ☐ black

☐ brown   ☐ pink

☐ blue   ☐ green

Guess the answers. Read and solve.

1.

You can see me in carrots, pumpkins, and autumn leaves. I am lighter than red. I am a kind of fruit, too.

Q: What color is it?   A: It's _____.

2.

You can see me in the sky on sunny days. You can also see me in the sea. I am all around in nature.

Q: What color is it?   A: It's _____.

3.

You can see me when you mix red and blue. Sometimes I am called violet.

Q: What color is it?   A: It's _____.

4.

You can see me in bananas or lemons. I am one of the bright and warm colors.

Q: What color is it?   A: It's _____.

The leaves are bright red, yellow, and orange.

 ## A Colorful Mountain

Emma and her father enjoy hiking on a beautiful day. Look and circle the color words.

"Can you see the snow on top of the mountain?" asks Emma.

"Yes, I can," says Dad. "What a beautiful view!"

Dad and Emma start the hike. The leaves are bright red, yellow, and orange. Brown squirrels run from tree to tree.

 ## B Read Again!

What color are the leaves? Answer the question.

_____

_____

A Opposite Hunt

Find the opposite word pairs. Look and write.

B What Color Is It?

Look and complete the sentences.

1.    I can ride my new _____ bike.

2.    My _____ helmet keeps my head safe.

3.    I put my _____ magic hat on my head.

C Opposite Bees

Look at the bees. They have opposite words! Read and write.

good

rich

light

low

D Odd One Out

Find the different word. Read and circle.

1. orange — pink — black — clean

2. heavy — yellow — good — clean

3. red — different — purple — brown

4. gray — long — short — fast

A Needle and Thread

Sew the torn clothes. Read and match.

1. We need some •   • favorite season.

2. I don't •   • milk and eggs.

3. Spring is my •   • like cucumbers.

4. What is your •   • favorite season?

B Back on Track

Look at the train off the track. Unscramble and write.

1. our grandmother.   We   are going to   see

2. season?   is   your   What   favorite

3. need   and eggs.   some milk   We

C Let's Renovate!

This building is so old. Find and write. Then rewrite the sentences.

1. I can _____ with the bees.

_____

2. The turnip falls on the _____ man.

_____

3. I have _____ hands.

_____

4. I have two small feet and _____ legs.

_____

5. The leaves are bright red, _____, and orange.

_____

Word Bank

old   short   fly   little   yellow

Family

me

1. grandmother ☐   2. father ☐   3. mother ☐

4. grandfather ☐   5. sister ☐   6. brother ☐

Weather & Seasons

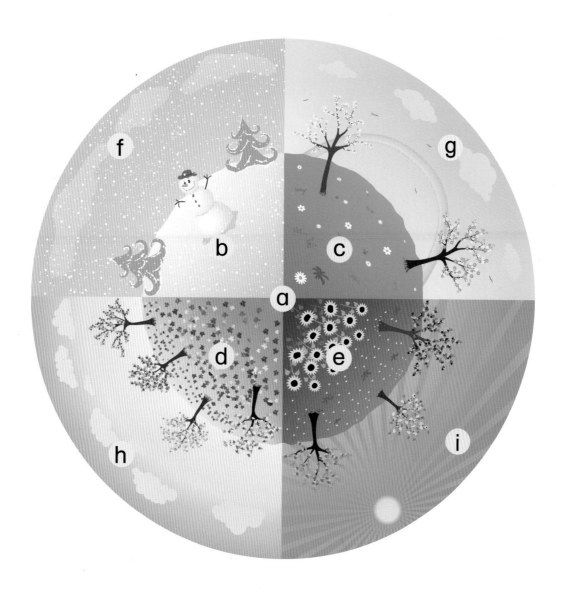

1. spring ☐ 2. fall ☐ 3. cool ☐

4. snowy ☐ 5. warm ☐ 6. winter ☐

7. summer ☐ 8. sunny ☐ 9. seasons ☐

Food

1. sandwich ☐   2. spaghetti ☐   3. yogurt ☐

4. bread ☐   5. chicken ☐   6. soup ☐

7. pizza ☐   8. egg ☐   9. hot dog ☐

Fruits & Vegetables

Fruits

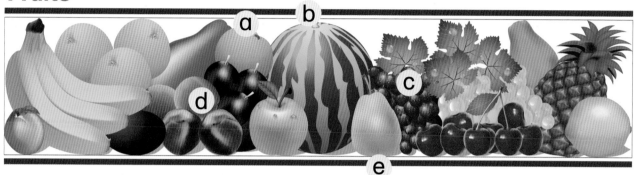

Vegetables

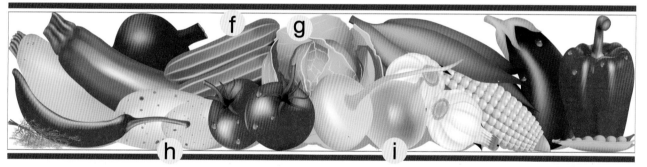

1. cabbage	☐	2. cucumber	☐	3. potato	☐
4. pear	☐	5. grapes	☐	6. peach	☐
7. watermelon	☐	8. onion	☐	9. orange	☐

Action Verbs

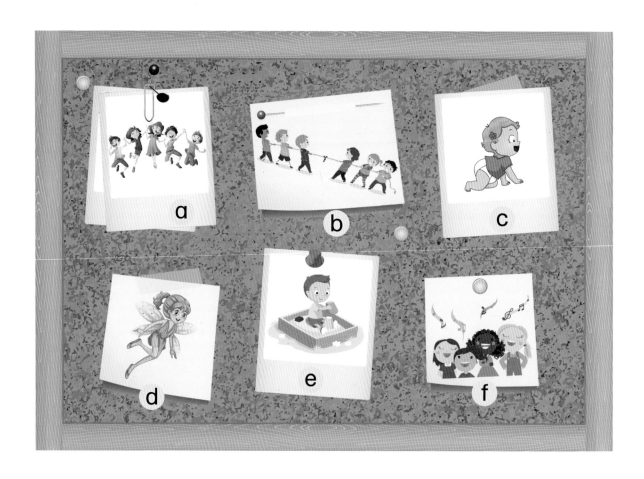

1. sit down ☐   2. crawl ☐   3. fly ☐

4. sing ☐   5. pull ☐   6. jump ☐

Appearance & People

1. girl ☐   2. fat ☐   3. weak ☐

4. beautiful ☐   5. strong ☐   6. handsome ☐

7. man ☐   8. thin ☐   9. woman ☐

Opposites

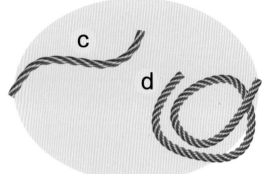

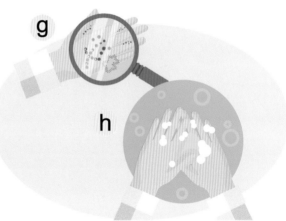

1. dirty   2. short   3. good ☐

4. bad ☐   5. long   6. clean ☐

7. big   8. little

Colors

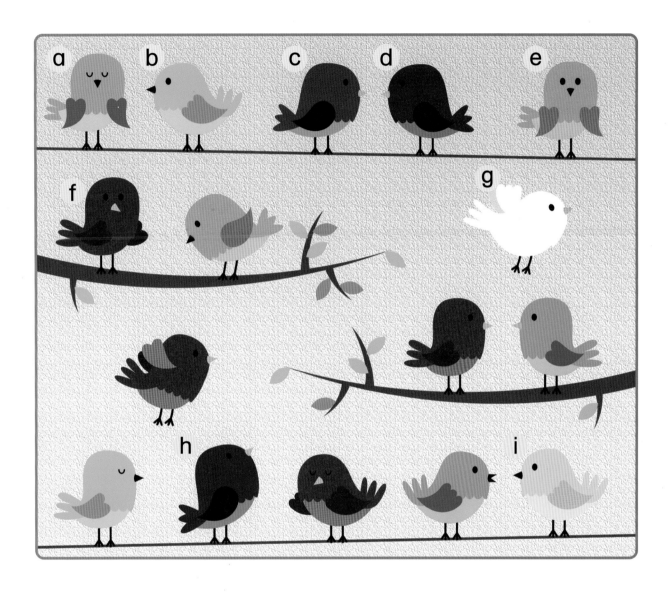

1. blue ☐ 2. brown ☐ 3. black ☐

4. purple ☐ 5. orange ☐ 6. white ☐

7. red ☐ 8. green ☐ 9. yellow ☐

1. Family

p.2
B 1. grandfather 2. grandmother
3. father 4. mother 5. brother 6. sister

p.3
C 1. son 2. parent 3. family 4. wife
5. husband 6. baby

p.4
D 1. grandmother 2. husband
3. daughter 4. parent 5. brother
6. cousin

p.5
A father, mother, sister, grandmother, grandfather
B We are going to see our grandmother and grandfather.

2. Weather & Seasons

p.6
B 1. spring 2. summer 3. rainy
4. sunny 5. fall 6. winter 7. windy
8. snowy

p.7
C 1. hot 2. spring 3. cloudy 4. sunny
D 1. cloudy 2. windy 3. sunny 4. rainy
5. stormy

p.8
E 1. winter 2. cloudy 3. windy
4. stormy 5. snowy

p.9
A 1. Spring 2. Summer 3. Fall 4. Winter

Review(1, 2)

p.10
A 1. weather 2. daughter 3. stormy
4. seasons 5. grandfather 6. cousin
B 1. son 2. snowy 3. cloudy 4. husband

p.11
C 2. grandmother ⇒ grandfather
3. uncles ⇒ sons 4. stormy ⇒ sunny

3. Food

p.12
B 1. sandwich 2. yogurt 3. cake 4. milk
5. spaghetti 6. cookie 7. rice 8. beef

p.13
C 1. pizza 2. soup 3. spaghetti
4. bread 5. rice 6. beef 7. chicken
8. cookie 9. yogurt

p.14
D 1. c 2. a 3. k 4. e / cake

p.15
A 1. a 2. b
B milk and eggs (eggs and milk)

4. Fruits & Vegetables

p.16
B 1. onion 2. cabbage 3. pear
4. melon 5. grapes

p.17
C 1. carrot 2. strawberry 4. grapes
5. cucumber 6. potato 8. watermelon

p.18
D
Fruits: banana, melon, strawberry, apple / Vegetables: pumpkin, cabbage, carrot, onion

p.19
A 1. Eat your vegetables. 2. I don't like cucumbers.
B I don't like cucumbers.

Review(3, 4)

p.20
A 1. cookies 2. spaghetti 3. sandwich
4. pizza
B 1. carrot 2. cabbage 3. peach
4. pear

p.21
C 1. rice 2. milk, egg 3. beef 4. apple

5. Action Verbs

p.22
B 1. fly 2. jump 3. crawl 4. stand up
5. sit down 6. pull 7. sing

p.23
C 1. c 2. f 3. b 4. a 5. e 6. d 7. g 8. h

p.24
D come / walk / crawl / point / go /
hop / stand up / run / eat

p.25
A can / cannot
B fly with the bees

6. Appearance & People

p.26
B 1. children 2. short 3. tall 4. old
5. young 6. girl 7. boy

p.27
C 1. noisy 2. woman 3. children
4. quiet
D 1. fat, thin 2. young 3. short, short

p.28
E 1. woman, man 2. boy, fly 3. girl, go
4. weak, weather 5. strong, long

p.29
A man, woman, girl
B The turnip falls on the old man.

Review(5, 6)

p.30
A 1. dance 2. point 3. crawl 4. come
5. noisy 6. chase
B 1. handsome 2. short / thin
3. pretty 4. tall / strong

p.31
C 1. crawl 2. drink 3. noisy 4. pull
5. point 6. tall

7. Opposites

p.32
B 1. fast 2. different 3. clean 4. little

p.33
C 1. rich 2. dirty 3. high 4. heavy

5. long 6. soft 7. tiny 8. bad

p.34
D 1. tiny / heavy / dirty 2. same /
slow / soft 3. huge / hard / high
4. light / little / low

p.35
A 1. short 2. little
B 1. I have short arms. 2. I have little hands.

8. Colors

p.36.
B 1. black 2. yellow 3. orange 4. blue
5. white 6. brown

p.37
C yellow, purple, red, green, orange, white
D gray, black, brown, pink, blue, green

p.38
E 1. orange 2. blue 3. purple 4. yellow

p.39
A red, yellow, orange, Brown
B The leaves are bright red, yellow, and orange.

Review(7, 8)

p.40
A fast-slow / same-different / huge-tiny
B 1. red 2. brown 3. yellow

p.41
C bad, poor, heavy, high
D 1. clean 2. yellow 3. different 4. gray

Expressions Review

p.42
A 1. milk and eggs. 2. like cucumbers.
3. favorite season. 4. favorite season?
B 1. We are going to see our grandmother.
2. What is your favorite season?
3. We need some milk and eggs.

p.43
C 1. fly 2. old 3. little 4. short 5. yellow

Picture Dictionary

p.44
1. b 2. d 3. e 4. a 5. c 6. f

p.45
1. c 2. d 3. h 4. f 5. g 6. b 7. e 8. i 9. a

p.46
1. a 2. h 3. d 4. e 5. f 6. i 7. b 8. c 9. g

p.47
1. g 2. f 3. h 4. e 5. c 6. d 7. b 8. i 9. a

p.48
1. e 2. c 3. d 4. f 5. b 6. a

p.49
1. i 2. a 3. f 4. d 5. e 6. c 7. h 8. b 9. g

p.50
1. g 2. c 3. b 4. a 5. d 6. h 7. e 8. f

p.51
1. a 2. c 3. h 4. d 5. e 6. g 7. f 8. b 9. i

Family

mother

Family

father

Family

family

Family

parent

Family

son

Family

brother

Family

sister

Family

daughter

Family

grandmother

Family

grandfather

Family

uncle

Family

aunt

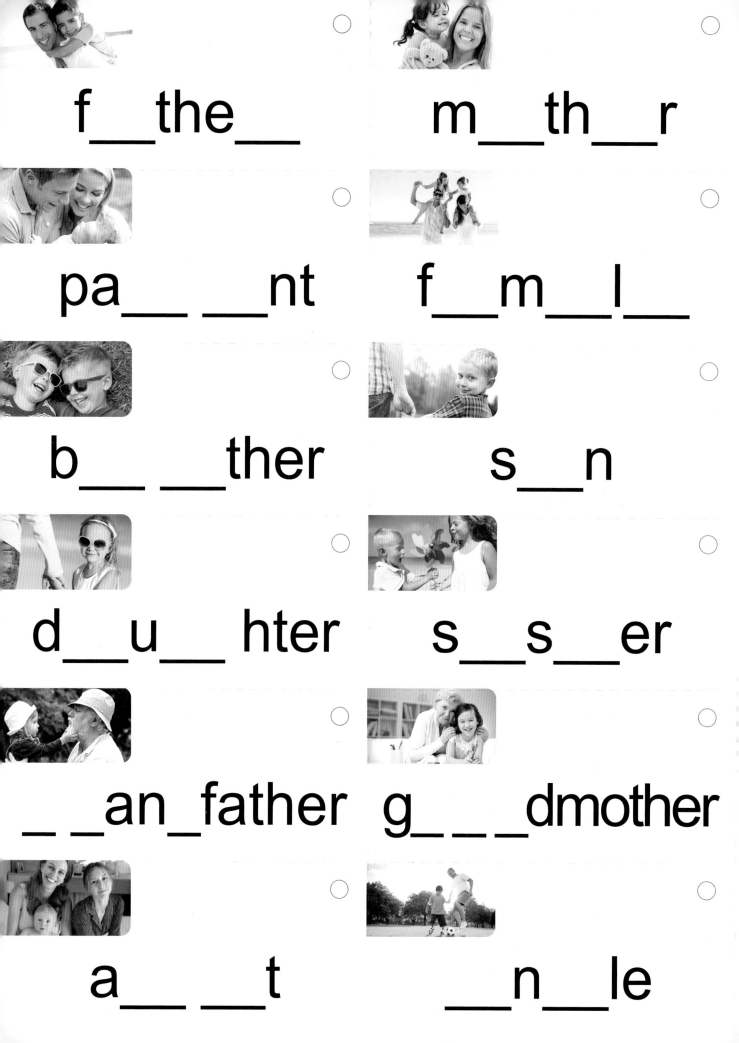

f__the__   m__th__r

pa____ __nt   f__m__l__

b__ __ther   s__n

d__u__hter   s__s__er

__ __an__father   g__ __ __dmother

a__ __t   __n__le

spring

summer

fall

winter

cold

hot

sunny

rainy

snowy

windy

cool

warm

su__m__r   __ __ __ing

w__ __ter   fa__ __

__o__   c__l__

r__ __ny   sun__ __

win__ __   __ __ __owy

w__ __m   c__ __l

Food	Food
milk	egg

Food	Food
bread	rice

Food	Food
cake	cookie

Food	Food
sandwich	beef

Food	Food
hot dog	pizza

Food	Food
soup	spaghetti

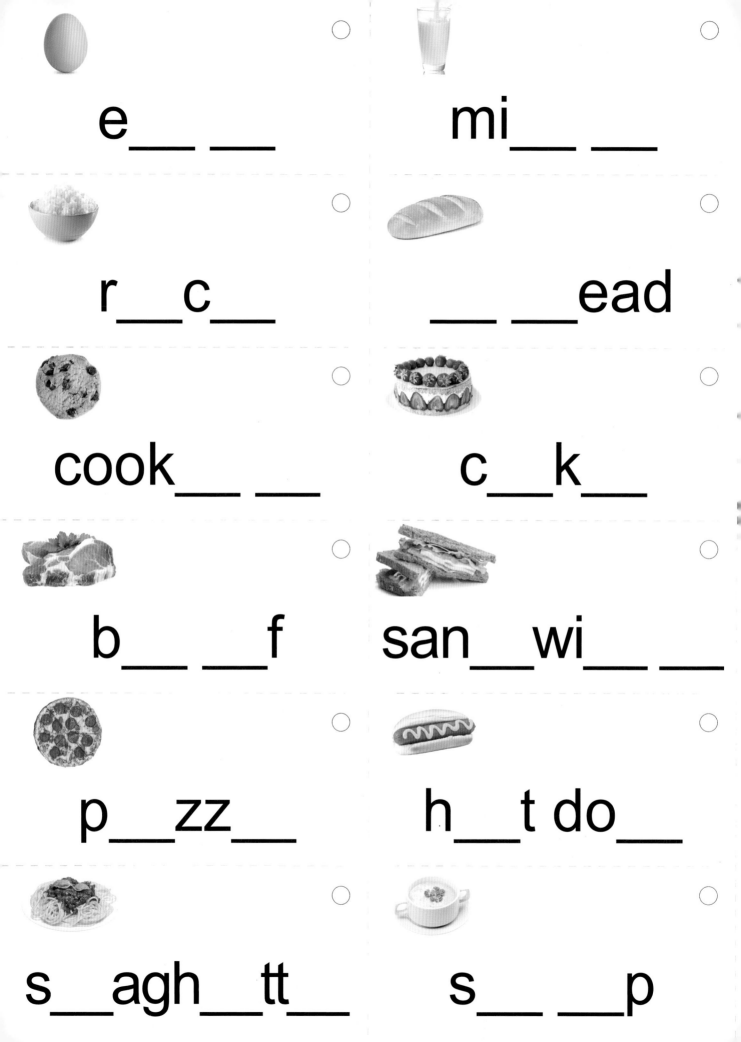

e__ __

mi__ __

r__c__

__ __ead

cook__ __

c__k__

b__ __f

san__wi__ __ __

p__zz__

h__t do__

s__agh__tt__

s__ __p

Fruits & Vegetables

apple

Fruits & Vegetables

orange

Fruits & Vegetables

banana

Fruits & Vegetables

strawberry

Fruits & Vegetables

watermelon

Fruits & Vegetables

grapes

Fruits & Vegetables

bean

Fruits & Vegetables

potato

Fruits & Vegetables

carrot

Fruits & Vegetables

cucumber

Fruits & Vegetables

onion

Fruits & Vegetables

pumpkin

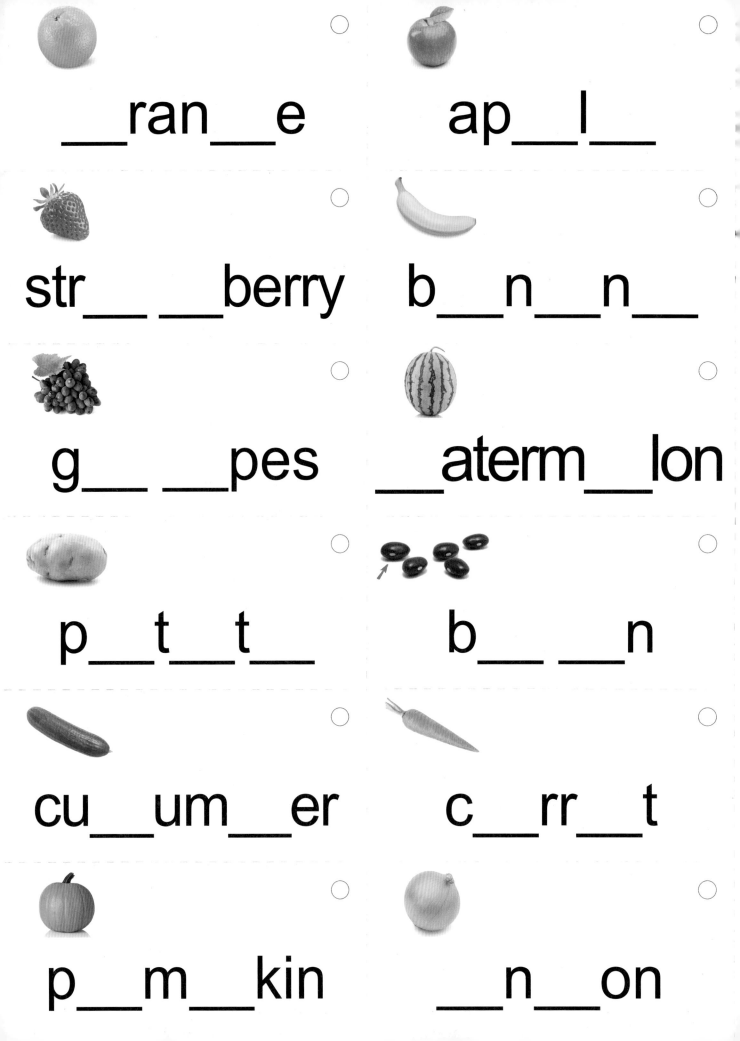

__ran__e

ap__l__

str__ __berry

b__n__n__

g__ __pes

__aterm__lon

p__t__t__

b__ __n

cu__um__er

c__rr__t

p__m__kin

__n__on

go

eat

run

walk

stand up

sit down

drink

jump

sing

kick

pull

push

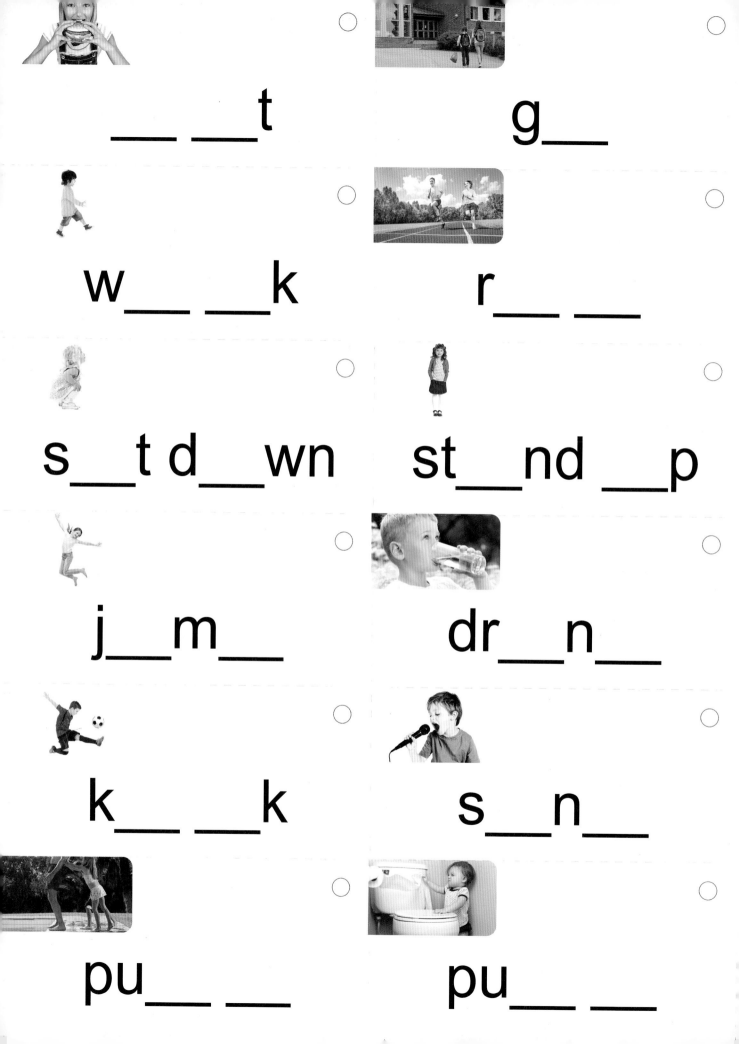

__ __t

g__

w__ __k

r__ __

s__t d__wn

st__nd __p

j__m__

dr__n__

k__ __k

s__n__

pu__ __

pu__ __

old

young

strong

weak

fat

thin

tall

short

beautiful

handsome

pretty

children

y__ __ng

o__ __

w__ __k

stro__ __

__ __in

f__ __ __

__ __ort

t__ __ l

h__nds__me

b__ __ __ __tiful

child__ __ __

pre__ __ __y

Opposites

good

Opposites

bad

Opposites

same

Opposites

different

Opposites

fast

Opposites

slow

Opposites

clean

Opposites

dirty

Opposites

hard

Opposites

soft

Opposites

poor

Opposites

rich

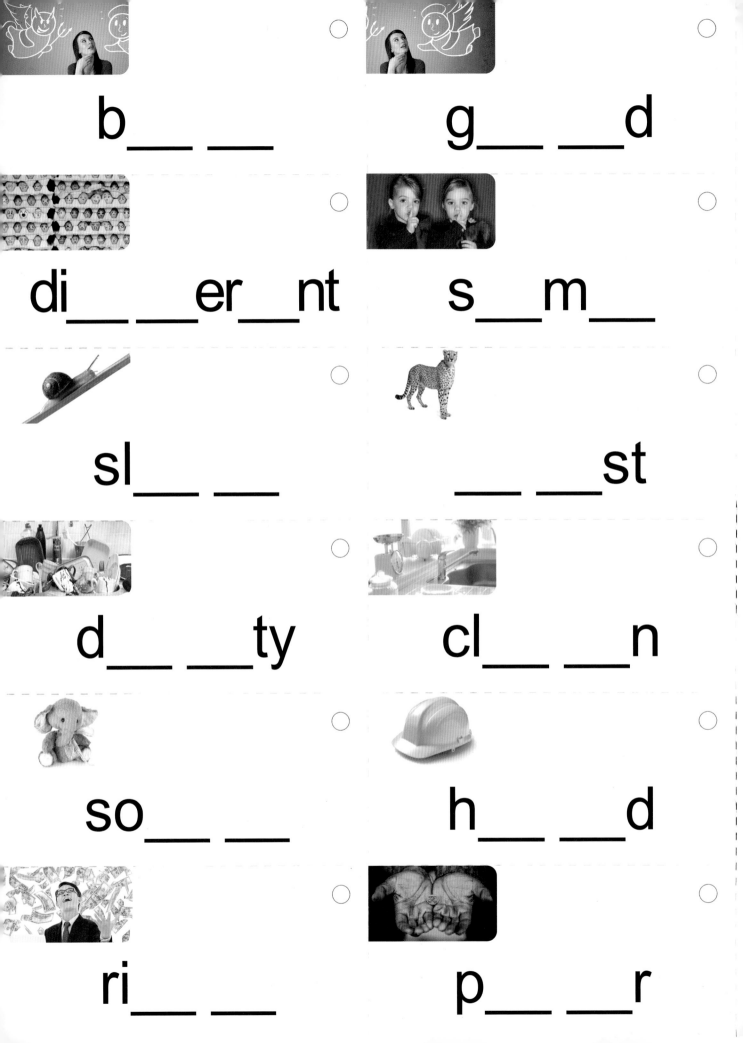

b__ __

g__ __d

di__ __er __nt

s__m__

sl__ __

__ __st

d__ __ty

cl__ __n

so__ __

h__ __d

ri__ __

p__ __r

white

black

red

green

blue

brown

yellow

orange

pink

purple

gray

colorful

__ __ack

__ __ite

__ __ __een

r__ __

br__ __n

bl__ __

__r__ng__

y__ll__w

p__ __ple

pi__ __

c__lor__ __l

g__ __y